*This book was donated through the...*

# Ben Carson Reading Room Grant

### March 1, 2004

WOODSIDE ELEMENTARY
MEDIA CENTER

# Get Out of My Chair

Written by Kathy Schulz
Illustrated by Tom Payne

Woodside Elementary School
Media Center

**⟨P⟩ Children's Press®**
A Division of Scholastic Inc.
New York • Toronto • London • Auckland • Sydney
Mexico City • New Delhi • Hong Kong
Danbury, Connecticut

To all of the shelter dogs and puppies
who await homes (and chairs!)
—K.S.

Reading Consultants
**Linda Cornwell**
Coordinator of School Quality and Professional Improvement
(Indiana State Teachers Association)

**Katharine A. Kane**
Education Consultant
(Retired, San Diego County Office of Education and San Diego State University)

Library of Congress Cataloging-in-Publication Data
Shulz, Kathy.
    Get out of my chair / written by Kathy Schulz ; illustrated by Tom Payne.
        p. cm. — (Rookie reader)
    Summary: A child and a dog fight for space on the same chair.
    ISBN 0-516-22350-X (lib. bdg.)          0-516-25965-2 (pbk.)
    [1. Dogs—Fiction. 2. Stories in rhyme.] I. Payne, Tom, ill. II. Title. III. Series.
PZ8.3.S2974 Ge 2001
[E]—dc21                                                          00-047372

# Get out of my chair.

Go on your way.

Get out of my chair.

You cannot stay.

Get out of my chair.
I am telling you.

Get out of my chair.
I will count to two.

Get out of my chair.
You must get down.

Get out of my chair,
you little clown.

Get out of my chair.
Listen, Rover!

19

Get out of my chair . . .

or scoot over.

23

# Word List (28 words)

| | | |
|---|---|---|
| am | little | stay |
| cannot | must | telling |
| chair | my | to |
| clown | of | two |
| count | on | way |
| down | or | will |
| get | out | you |
| go | over | your |
| I | Rover | |
| listen | scoot | |

 ## About the Author

Kathy Schulz is an elementary school teacher with a great love for animals—especially dogs. She enjoys taking walks with Baxter, her twelve-year-old dog, and often volunteers at a local animal shelter. *Get Out of My Chair* was inspired by the antics of the dogs and puppies in her life.

 ## About the Illustrator

Tom Payne has been a humorous illustrator for a very long time. His work has appeared in all sorts of books and magazines. He commutes into his studio, which he shares with some other "arty" people, in Albany, New York, from his home in the nearby Helderberg Mountains. He lives with his wife, Anne, and his sons, Thomas and Matthew.